DADDILESS DAUGHTERS

Copyright © 2017 by Solomon & Makeda Inc.

All Rights Reserved. No parts of this book may be reproduced in any form without the express written consent of Publisher/Authors, except in the case of brief quotations embodied within relevant articles and book reviews for print ad electronic media.

Table of Contents

Preface – How I See God "My little g God" ……………..I

Intro – Daddy's Girl …………………………………......V

Chapter 1 – What is a Daddiless Daughter?........................1

Chapter 2 – Self-Esteem "My Reinforcement"…………...6

Chapter 3 – Teen Dating & Promiscuity "My Standard Setter"………………………………………………….......11

Chapter 4 – Finances "My Provider"………………..…...18

Chapter 5 – Careers and Goals "My Coach"…………..…22

Chapter 6 – Adult Relationships – "My Intervener"……..28

Chapter 7 – Marriage "My Exchanger"…………………..35

Epilogue……………………………………………....….41

References…………………………………………...……

Preface

How I see God

"My little g god"

Every good and perfect gift is from above comes down from the Father of lights... (James 1:17)

...But you have received the spirit of adoption by whom we cry out "Abba (daddy) Father" (Rom. 8:15)

I believe it is the design of God to have earthy fathers that point us in the direction of our Heavenly Father! The way you view your natural or earthly father could very much affect the way you view God. Many people have no problem identifying God as a higher power, a deity or even a supernatural being, but many struggle with the concept of seeing him as their father.

A father's job is not just to protect and provide but also to love and have relationship with their children. The problem is if you can't comprehend natural things, how could you possibly comprehend spiritual things?

In my own life, as I began to develop a stronger relationship with my daddy, I started to really see God the Father that way. One day me and all 3 of my siblings had planned to visit my dad and he was so excited about it he could hardly wait! He called me the day before the visit and I could hear the excitement in his voice, and he said, "I need you all to get here early we have so many things to discuss". Just like the Father (God), he was saying come let us reason together. When we finally arrived, he had let his full, grey beard out (which he never does). I thought to myself, he is showing us the wisdom and patience he has collected over the years. We talked about many things, the plans he had for us as a family and how it was his desire for his children to be closer. That's just like God I thought! He wants all of us to grow in love for one another and he always has a plan for us. I could give you many instances where my dad's affectionate display of love, his patience and wisdom would give me a deeper visual of God himself.

You see, God put it in the man to be a reflection of Himself; not just as the head, but as a good father. But unfortunately, there are many women and men alike that can't grasp this picture! Here are a few examples of how the image of God can be distorted in you:

➢ If you had a father, but he wasn't the type to communicate, he never really asks about your day or what was going on with you. You may not

see the benefit of praying to the Father and actually getting a response.
- ➢ If you didn't have a father in your life at all, you may question whether you are a child of God, or even worse whether God really exist.
- ➢ If you had an abusive father, whether emotionally or physically, you may think that God is mad at you and doesn't love you.
- ➢ If you had a father who didn't acknowledge you unless you did good; you may think that God only loves you when you are doing good. Maybe you feel like if you don't pray or do all the religious requirements of faith that God is not proud to call you his own.
- ➢ If your father was just a human bank, he provided for you financially, but he was never around; you might see God that way. You may only seek him when you need something, but when all is going well you don't really need him.

Before we came from the loins of our father in the earth, we came out of God himself. We are always on his heart and he knew us before he formed us in our mother's womb (Jer. 1:5). Our true identity is actually locked inside of him! Perhaps that is why we take on the last name of our father! Your natural father gives you language for who you are, what kind of family you come from and he even gives you his name. The same is true with God. He gives us language for who we are: he knows the plans he has for us, thoughts of peace and not evil, to give us hope and a future (Jer. 29:11). He tells us that we come from a Royal Family in heaven: "our citizenship is in heaven" (Phil. 3:20). And he has called us by name and declares that we are his (Isa. 43:1)!

Fathers, I hope you realize that you are more than just a sperm donor, you have literally been given the responsibility to be the "little g" god, to your family and your children.

Those who feel that it is too late to cultivate a relationship with their father for any reason, be encouraged and know that he is a father to the fatherless! You literally have a Father in heaven who loves you dearly. He has your name written in the palm of His hand and he knows every little detail about your life, even how many hairs you have on your head.

This is probably the most significant and most relevant purpose for a father. Above all else and I pray that you can see God as your daddy! Remember, every good and perfect gift (that's you) comes down from the Father of lights. He is the Father of lights and we are lights in this world!

Blessings, Grace and Peace.

Introduction

Daddy's Girl

I'll never forget the morning my daddy was arrested. At the tender age of 10 years old, a 5th grader, a little girl was forced to experience the pain of not having her dad around anymore. That morning I had injured my leg at school, so my mom came to pick me up and take me to my dad's house. When we arrived, to our surprise he WASN'T THERE! We soon found out that he was arrested and in my 10-year-old mind, I thought, he will be home soon. Soon wasn't so soon at all and from that point on I wouldn't see my dad on this side of freedom as a little girl ever again. I didn't realize that the whole trajectory of my life would change. I wouldn't be able to spend weekends at his house anymore, no more vacations to Jamaica, just me and him. He would miss all the highlights of my young life like awards ceremonies, graduations and my first "date". I would also lose my main source of financial support. At 10 I lost my daddy to the United States prison system.

I am grateful to have had an amazing father. For the years I did have him as a child, he was the definition of a daddy, and I was without a doubt a daddy's girl. He cooked for me, took me wherever I wanted to go, even places I didn't want to go, like his job! He bought me things, gave me allowances and taught me many things. He taught me the value of hard work, being kind to others and saving my money. He even let me sit on his lap and steer a dump truck while he worked the gas and break. I write this book because I know what it feels like to be a daddy's girl and I also know how it is to be a Daddiless daughter.

In the United States, approximately 21.2 million children are raised in a single parent household, about 84 percent of these children are raised by single mothers. That means there are millions of boys and girls that are growing up without a father at home. In a talk with Oprah Winfrey, Iyana Vanzant refers to women who grew up without fathers as "Daddiless Daughters"; which is where I got my title from. Fathers play a major role in the lives of their daughters whether absent or present. The fact is girls benefit from having fathers around, and on the contrary, there are consequences for not having a dad in their life. Dads are the complete package in parenting, they are there to compensate for the things that a mother can't give. It takes a mother's nurture and care but also a father's love and guidance. Whether or not a father is present in their daughter's life they are still shaping their views about life, men and relationships. A father's presence can affirm a daughter, make her feel secure, make her feel more confident, teach her about boys and give her the purest love between a man and a woman. On the contrary in a father's absence, whether emotional or physical, a girl is learning things like mistrust, abandonment, grief, low self-esteem and may look for love in all the wrong places. Childhood is something that can't be repeated, but often women who we call Daddiless daughters live with the wounds of not being raised with a father.

Are the issues faced by not having a father a life sentence? What does having a father really have to do with major life decisions? Do fathers play a role in their daughter's marriage? These are all questions that I hope to answer, in the chapters ahead!

Father's, if you have a daughter sill in childhood, take the time to reach out to her and connect with her! Time being a real dad to your daughter is NEVER time wasted. Just being around her, you are teaching her valuable lessons that only a daddy can teach. Some of these lessons can't necessarily be taught with words, but with action. The way you treat her, the love you show her, even the discipline you give is teaching her.

Mothers, don't keep your young daughters away from their father (if you are not together), no matter how good or bad you think he is. I thank God, my mother never told me anything her and my dad went through when I was a child. I never knew why they were divorced and she never painted any negative pictures in my head about him. She made sure to take

VIII

me to visit my dad in prison whenever she could. My mom had it right as a single mother raising girls! Maybe it was because she herself was a Daddiless daughter after her daddy died of a brain aneurism when she was a teenager. Mothers, I can't urge you enough! Don't keep your daughters away from their dad, no matter how "dead beat" you think he is, unless of course he has the potential to harm his own kid. In the long run, you daughter will thank you for giving her the opportunity to know her dad in a positive light.

Dedication

I would like to dedicate this book to two very important people to me:

To "the first man to ever hold me", my daddy, Donald G. Young.

To the real MVP, the one who stood in the gap and made up the hedge, my mommy, Patricia D. Russ.

I love you both dearly and I'm grateful to God that he chose you both to be my parents and me to be your daughter.

I would also like to send a special thanks to all my family and friends for all their love and support and to the men incarcerated at FCI Miami for inspiring me to make this happen!

CHAPTER ONE

What is a "Daddiless Daughter"?

The answer to this question is really not as simple as we would guess. While most people would say a Daddiless daughter is simply someone who is without a father, the answer is a little more intricate than that. Throughout this book, we will discover that there is a difference between a father and a daddy. Let's take a look at some those differences.

A Father

My own personal definition of a father is someone who simply fathered you. Some people call them "sperm donors". Don't get me wrong, fathers are still very important to us, we need to come out of somebody's loins in order to be born into this world. Webster's definition of father is "a. a male parent".

Something I found to be interesting is the woman that says I had a daddy, but I just never knew my biological father. Once I had a talk with a close friend of mine and she was contemplating whether she should find out who her real dad was after all these years. She had been raised by her great aunt and uncle, and he uncle was the daddy she knew and everything a girl could ever ask for. It wasn't until after his death that we had this talk. "Should I find out who my real dad was?" Her conviction was, I had the perfect dad and I feel bad for even wanting to know who my biological father is. Here was my answer, "I think you should definitely find him, not that you are looking for a daddy all over again as an adult, but your father is just as important as your daddy was. He may not have raised you, he may not even be half the man your uncle was, but you at least want to know who and where you came from."

A Daddy

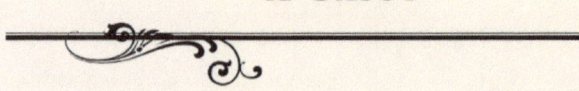

Again, my own personal definition of a daddy is someone who not only fathered you, which is important, but a male with whom you have an intimate connection with. Interestingly enough when I looked up the definition of "daddy" the first term that popped up was a "sugar daddy". Sugar daddy is defined as a generous benefactor of a cause. A generous benefactor is someone who lends their support, especially financially to a cause. The cause that your benefactor (daddy) should be supporting is your life. You see, a daddy is supposed to add sweetness into the lives of their children.

The term daddy's girl is used to describe a little girl who loves her dad and would give up almost anything to be with him and to make him proud. At a young age, girls begin to have an opposite attraction to their fathers and may even compete with their mother for their father's attention according to Sigmund Fraud. Fathers affirm their daughters and teach them what it means to be a girl from a man's perspective. Even early on fathers are teaching their young female children what it means to be loved and how to trust. With this in mind, one must consider, what happens to little girls who have never known their dad? Daddiless daughters are more likely to experience low self-esteem and behavioral challenges, lower academic and athletic achievement and poverty. We will discuss these concepts in later chapters.

Many people who have not been properly fathered don't necessarily use the term daddy when referring to their fathers. Instead it more of "that's my dad" or "he is my father". Many women around the world have yet to develop a relationship intimate enough with their dad to call him daddy. The good thing about a daddy is, he doesn't necessarily have to be the man that fathered you, although that is ideal.

When you are a child it is almost second nature to call your father daddy, but as we mature into adolescence that confession may change to just simply "dad". What happens during those critical years of life can really change the word by which we use to describe our male parent. In our adult years, the name we have called them by the most, will be the one we most often refer to him as. Whenever I meet a mature woman and she talks about her dad, if she calls him daddy; I can pretty much tell that she honors, loves and respects her dad.

The concept of father and daddy isn't necessarily set in stone. This terminology can vary based on culture, ethnicity, nationality and so on. It may be more reverential for you to call him dad, father, papa, papi etc. Whatever term carries more intimacy based on your personal experiences is who we deem daddy and the less intimate one we will call father. Although throughout the course of this book we will use the terms somewhat interchangeably.

There are also women who never knew their father, or their father is deceased. In that case, you could think of daddy or father as the most influential male role model in your life.

Women, I would like you to take a moment to think about which term comes to mind when you think of the man that put life in your mother's womb or the man who raised you.

Fathers, take a minute to reflect on what your daughter (no matter what age she is) calls you when she talks to you or about you.

CHAPTER TWO

Self Esteem

"Daddy the Counteractor"

As I grew into my adult years, it has really been a priority of mine to boost my self-esteem and redeem the years I spent not liking myself. I hated to look at myself in the mirror, I hated the way my voice sounded and forget about taking pictures! Most of my life I thought that something was wrong with me. Why didn't I like myself? Why couldn't I express myself like the other girls did? I was extremely shy, timid and unsure of myself. I remember in middle school when I got my first pair of contact lenses, I looked at myself straight in the eye for the first time in my life. Wait a minute I have pretty brown eyes I thought to myself! I had no idea! Who knew that behind the glasses, hearing aids and braces there was a beautiful young lady. From that moment forward, I started a slow and steady journey upward to find my own beauty rather than admiring what I seen in other people.

To my surprise, I wasn't alone in this struggle. Many women have never really dealt with their self-esteem issues. It may be subtle like masking behind make up, weave and lashes or it might be as extreme hating the way you look in the mirror all together. I'm not saying there is anything wrong with makeup, weave or lashes, but if you are using it as mask; to cover up what you don't like, it may be a problem! Maybe your self-esteem issues manifest by craving attention, or being over competitive, or being envious of what others have because you think what you have isn't good enough. Some people post their whole lives on social media, but could it be a cry for validation and attention? You may think I'm drawing some sharp conclusions, but I'm just simply presenting some possibilities that may or may not apply to you. Like the saying goes "If the shoe fits wear it". Own up to it so that you can do something about it. The deeper reality is somewhere along the line where someone has told us a lie about ourselves. "You look like this…" "You sound like this…" "You don't have this…" "She looks better…" "You can't do this…" THEY say. Maybe people have even told you that you're ugly or stupid. Those words never went anywhere if you never dealt with them, they simply concealed themselves in your personality. These unconfronted words have morphed you into somebody "THEY" wanted you to be, but really who are you? Here is the truth, you are not what THEY said about you. You may be wondering, what does this have to do with my dad?

  Here is another important role daddy's play in their daughter's life. They should rebound the negativity of others and reinforce this with the positive by telling you, you are beautiful, smart and valuable. Daddy should be your *counteractor*. Here is a healthy example of this. A girl comes home from school and dad ask about her day. She should naturally be able to communicate with him what hurt her, what made her upset or what the kids said about her at school and more importantly how she felt about it. His response should be something like "don't listen to them (rebound), you're beautiful (reinforce) and I love you. Maybe even add a joking remark like, "do I need to come to that school?". Its conversations like these that will not only boost self-confidence, but it will teach girls how to deal with unavoidable conflict and rise above it.

There are many dangers in a girl with low self-esteem. It opens the door for low standards as it pertains to relationships, to educational and career choices, and even self-image. These are all areas that make for a healthy woman, and yet these are the very areas that low self-esteem attacks. I took the time to look up the definition of self-esteem and it means confidence in one's own worth or abilities, self-respect. Low self-esteem can affect the things we accomplish, people we interact with and most importantly our relationship with ourselves. While I'm not implying that absent dads are the sole reason for low self-esteem, I am indicating that a healthy relationship with a father is an antidote.

In a later chapter, we will be discussing relationships and marriage. One thing is certain you can't love others until you love yourself. "Love your neighbor as yourself" is a quote we all know and even repeat but do we really understand the power in this command? Basically, you only have the ability to love your neighbor as much as you love yourself. So, if you only like yourself, worse if you don't, you can't truly love others!

You may be thinking well, I didn't have a counteractor or it's too late for those kinds of prep talks. Ladies here is my encouragement: you should be proud that you made it this far in life without it, now it's time to pick up the pieces and build yourself up! You are beautiful, and you are loved, and you absolutely matter!

To the fathers that feel like it's too late for them to make a difference, it's not! Whether your daughter is 4 or 74 or anywhere in between, your words of encouragement, affirmation and love have so much power. They have the power to negate everything that "THEY" said.

Lastly, since we are talking about counteractors I would like to encourage you to take time to know and understand how God feels about you. In my quest to build my self-esteem NOTHING helped me more than the words my heavenly Father has spoken about me! He said that I am fearfully and wonderfully made, He told me that He created me in His image and in His likeness, He said I am the head and not the tail and that I am accepted in the beloved! He is the great Creator, EVERYTHING He ever created was good, including you!

CHAPTER THREE

Teen Dating and Promiscuity

"My Standard Setter"

In this chapter, we will discuss teen dating and promiscuity, and I myself will be as transparent as possible in order for you, as a reader, to directly connect with this topic. Then I will share some information based on my own research of the topic.

A Personal Testament

As a child, my mother was in a very emotionally abusive relationship. Reality is I've spent many nights as a child crying myself to sleep as I listened to my mom being verbally abused by her boyfriend. I remember many nights my mom would come lay with me, with a face covered in tears just to avoid further conflict with her drunken lover. I went to school many days after having cried myself to sleep and I wondered, where was my dad? As an elementary school child, I believe I hid my pain by excelling in school and being on my best behavior all the time! I was the kid who never acted out, never got mad, one who most would call a "goodie two shoes". Around about middle school, I started to bury myself in the internet making friends all over the world. I began to involve myself in puppy love online relationships. My friends at the time all had boyfriends and they were doing things I only thought about, while I was sitting at home on the internet. Then one day I decided I want that too! While I was never able to muster up the courage to do the things they did, I was determined to fit into the click. When I was 16 I got exactly what I was searching for, I met a guy that showed me the smallest amount of attention and we began to date. He was older than I was, and often pressured me about getting intimate with him. Finally, at 17 I decided I was old enough and it happened. A sense of profound grief fell over me and I truly regretted it, it was not a pleasurable experience for me at all! This is not what I had imagined! Long story short a few weeks later he called me and said he had a baby on the way by another girl! Surprisingly, I wasn't in the least way devastated. A few days later I met another guy and we began to date. He too was older than I was but at least he seemed to like me around. After a while he started to become possessive and always wanted me to be with him. Well, soon after our relationship started I was off to college. We tried the whole long-distance thing, until one day I called him, and another girl answered his phone! Here we go again I thought! Yet again, a few days later I met another guy who worked on campus at my school. That lasted for a while until I was met with more lies! After him, I met ANOTHER guy and that was by far the longest and most toxic relationship I have had. We were together six years, I was lied to, stolen from, emotionally battered, depressed and caused my family and friends a lot of heart ache. I have spared you a lot of the details but as you can see this was a continual cycle. It really started from a mother doing the best she could in a desperate situation and a father who.... you guessed it WASN'T THERE! Please bear in mind I had opportunities to reach out to my mom, or communicate these things with my dad, but I was a confused teen and a Daddiless daughter!

Taken Directly from Research

"The lack of parental involvement has been found to contribute to youth creating bonds with deviant peers that can result in sexual activity. Adolescents attempt to meet their needs by creating bonds that may be absent in their family structure" (Rowlette, 2013). As mentioned previously, girls without fathers suffer a loss of love and they often search for that love in other places. Mothers who are emotionally healthy and mature can help to alleviate some of these issues, but in the absence of the right support from a mother, girls will look to boyfriends and lovers (Thomas, 2012). In situations where there is a single mother, most times she is giving ALL that she has, but all that she has may not be sufficient enough for a Daddiless daughter. So, there is sort of a chain reaction taking place: if the father doesn't give the love a daughter needs, she can get it from a healthy relationship with her mother, and when the mother can't give it, for whatever reason, she will look to dating relationships to fulfil that need for a father's love.

One article I found on this subject says that girls who have a secure, supportive, communicative relationship with their dad are less likely to become sexually active in their early years (Nelson, 2014). For a Daddiless daughter it's more likely for them to conform to their partner sexually in effort to maintain the relationship. In a sense, girls without daddies experience a greater pressure from significant others to have sex as a means to keep the relationship. Although sex doesn't make the situation better, for a Daddiless daughter any form of attention from a male counterpart is better than none. "If a woman has a good relationship with her father, she is less likely to be on a quest for male approval or seek male affection through promiscuous sex" (Jackson, 2010). A young woman without a dad has a heart that is searching for genuine and intimate love. That kind of love can be easily mistaken for sex, without a clear definition of what love is and how it feels.

Eventually this quest to find love through sexual relationships will lead to a dead end with more feelings of grief, loss and low self-esteem. This may land a girl in the hands of another man who will abandon her, and then another and the cycle just continues. Being promiscuous is defined as having many sexual relationships. Promiscuity is the result of having searched for love through sex and not finding it in one person, so the search for love through sex continues. "Females without father figures often become desperate for male attention" (Mancini, 2010). Also, an insert on promiscuous behavior, research has shown that about 60 percent of female exotic dancers had absent fathers (Rowlette, 2013). This is just a real-life statistic of how absent fathers affect the promiscuity of their daughters.

So how do girls find themselves in promiscuous situations?

The first reason we have already discussed which is a search for a father's love. The second reason could possibly be mirroring the mother's behavior. Often times single mothers in a quest to find a suitable mate for themselves and their children will date many men. When a daughter is exposed to this they may mimic this behavior, not realizing that the reasoning is totally different! A mother is in search for a suitable partner, while a teen daughter is just simply in search for a love that has gone missing (Mancini, 2010). In my own experience with dating, as a teen, I realize now that the boys I dated were NOTHING like my dad, but they actually were very similar to my mom's boyfriend.

One of the results of living a promiscuous lifestyle is teenage pregnancy. "...Girls whose fathers left the family earlier in their lives had the highest rates of both early sexual activity and adolescent pregnancy. There are many reasons why this statistic stands as a fact in today's society. Mirroring their mother's behavior is probably the most obvious. Another speculation is that Daddiless daughters go through personality changes at a young age that makes them more likely to interact with males. It's interesting to note that a study showed that girls without fathers sit closer to men and interact with them more than girls who had fathers. The study also concluded that the longer a child was without a father the earlier she started her menstrual cycle. So, another possible explanation for teen pregnancy among Daddiless daughters is the fact that a father's absence could trigger hormonal changes, that jumpstart puberty and thus lead to earlier sexual activity and unplanned pregnancies.

As you can see, there is much to be said about this particular topic! As you look into your own life, can you see this topic as relevant to yourself or maybe a girlfriend, a wife or even your own daughter? This is a no judgement zone of course, but maybe it will help you to heal from your past or help you to help someone else heal. Take a moment to apply this information directly to yourself and those around you!

CHAPTER FOUR

Finances

"My Provider"

"A good man leaves an inheritance for his children's children"

They say money is the root of all evil, but I would like to suggest to you that money answers all things! I remember when I went to the hearing doctor and I found out that my hearing had gotten really bad, they told me if I didn't get hearing aids soon my brain would stop recognizing certain sounds. I looked at my mom in tears and she insisted we get a price for some hearing aids. The doctor gave a price of little over 3 thousand dollars and I felt hopeless. We left the doctor, but my mom was determined to make it happen. When she told my dad, he called me on the phone and said, "I've just mailed out 500 dollars to you towards your hearing aids". I stood there in tears thinking my dad is in prison and he sent ME 500 dollars! Two things ran through my mind. First, I thought he is definitely a provider. Second, if this man, my daddy could do this for me in prison, I had absolutely NO business with a man who had his freedom that couldn't do the same for me! What a life changing moment! Among the many people to donate were my mom's oldest brother and my pastor. I had come to the conclusion that I had real men in my life that were willing to contribute to my wellbeing. Financial provision is not just the role of a father, but it also allows them to prove to their children, and in this context to their daughters, that they are valuable. It's simply a daddy telling his daughter "you are worthy of my sacrifice".

    Many working-class women totally disagree that today's men still manage to make more money doing the same work. I actually think it's right, even though I myself am a working-class woman. Here is my reasoning: men, fathers, husbands are supposed to be using those extra resources to provide for their families. The real problem is, we have got too many single mothers, too many irresponsible daddies and the family structure is distorted.

I'm sure it's not surprising to you that Daddiless daughters are at a greater risk for poverty as compared to girls with fathers. I would like to present two possible explanations among many. The first which is most obvious is a lack of additional income and the mother having to pull the whole load. The second is more of a cause and effect. Due to the lack of academic and emotional support from fathers we see an increased risk for unplanned pregnancy, and increased high school, and even college dropout rates. These variables could affect a woman's ability to produce a decent income in the long term. How different would life be if every family had a father that helped fund their child's education and gave them a portion of their inheritance once they started life as an adult. We would eliminate generational poverty, get rid of debt and produce more professionals to solve world problems. Wishful thinking of course, but it goes to show how a providing father can start a chain reaction to bring about world change.

I have been in private Christian school most of my life, which is not cheap! I visited the white house in middle school. I have flown first class many times as a child. I never went without clothes, food or shelter. I never went one Christmas without several gifts under the tree. Most people who really know me would call me spoiled but not a brat. In high school, I participated in every activity I wanted to, and when it was time for college I was awarded a 20-thousand-dollar scholarship. All of this with a single parent mother and an incarcerated father. If you were to ask me how all this was possible I would say my Daddy in heaven is my ultimate Provider. He supplies all my needs according to his riches in glory. He is a rewarder to those that diligently seek him. Most importantly he has given me an inheritance! I don't have a need, or a want for that matter, that he won't supply. If you feel that you don't have the financial support, you need as a daughter (or a son) always remember to look up!

CHAPTER FIVE

Careers and Goals

"My Coach"

I remember when I first got accepted into undergrad at the University of South Florida. In high school, my dream was to have my dad be present at my high school graduation, but of course that didn't happen. My next goal was to have my dad be there when I walk the stage to get my first college degree. During my experience in undergrad, I met many girls my age that have become great friends of mine. I couldn't help but notice the family structure of my girlfriends in college. Many of them had come from what I would call, picture perfect families with a mom, dad, siblings and a "dog name spot". That was far from the reality I was facing, and I was often a shame to talk about my dad or where he was. One of my closest friends at USF had an amazing family, a supportive dad, a loving mother and a cool little brother. I really admired her drive and also her confidence. I began to wonder to myself, how come my life isn't quite fitting together like hers, not in a jealous way but in a way of general curiosity. Her dad would call every morning when we went to the gym and give her pointers about working out. She had a very open relationship with her father and they talked about everything from sex to school. I hadn't realized it then, but I knew there was a correlation between her being confident in everything she did and her daddy being her "life coach". We were both involved in a community service organization, my friend was the president and I was vice president. Together we set goals to do well in our classes, to get healthy and to be actively involved on campus and the surrounding community. I'm grateful for her friendship, she taught me a lot. The most important lesson I learned is how beneficial a daddy can be. Today she is a Licensed therapist, doing very well for herself, she graduated on time, started a great career and family, and has checked off many goals on her check list. If I were to be totally transparent, sometimes I wonder how much further along my own life would be if I had my daddy? Contrary to my friend, I started college not knowing exactly what career to purse, not having enough financial support and not having my daddy around. In my junior year I began my toxic relationship with my ex-boyfriend. My life began to spiral downward, my involvement on campus diminished, my goals slowly began to disappear. Before I knew it, I was sitting in my apartment depressed every day, failing all my classes, fired from my part time job on campus and with a toxic lover who had no motivation himself. That year, my junior year, I lost sight of everything…and if I'm really honest, I don't remember having one conversation with my dad. My parents had no idea what was going on, and at that point I certainly didn't want them to know.

   You see, affirmation is defined as emotional support or encouragement. It is not just a father's job to love you, provide and protect but also to affirm you. When I think about some of the world's leading women, not all but many have father's that were in their corner cheering them on. We see this in many arena's where women lead, in sports, in arts and entertainment, religious leaders, and even your everyday hero's like teachers, lawyers, doctors and the like. Not only do you know the gift they are to the world, but you also know their daddies. A few examples that come to mind are women like Venus and Serena, Beyoncé', Janet Jackson, Dr. Juanita Bynum. In the context of this discussion, girls who had actively engaged fathers that encouraged them are more likely to succeed in grade school, graduate college, and land jobs that are typical for men in society. "Today's fathers also seem to have a greater impact on their daughters academic and career choices than fathers in previous generations (Nelson, 2014). A possible explanation for their academic achievement is that fathers encourage daughters to take on subjects that women are generally not good at. One of these subjects for example, is mathematics which is generally associated with masculinity. A girl with a supportive dad has a bit of an advantage. Women are discouraged from going into certain fields of study, and girls who don't have dads may be more likely to succumb to this discouragement. "…Lack of encouragement can stem from feeling unprotected by their fathers, and they may feel insecure, even when it comes to their future education" (Mancini, 2010). There is no definite why, when it comes to why Daddiless daughters fall short in the area of career and goals. The best way to view it is, a boxer after having fought a tough round goes back to his corner to break, and there is NO COACH. No water boy, no one to cater to your wounds, no encouragement, no "you can do it" pep talks. Daddiless daughters are that boxer and daddy is supposed to be the coach waiting in the corner, but for many he is not.

    I moved back home in my senior year, to finish my classes online. During that time, I began to connect with my dad. I visited him more often and he started to call me once a week. To my surprise our visits together became my inspiration to do better. My dad became my motivator and he would encourage me to not only do well in school, but also to think like an entrepreneur. Listening to my dad's motivation and his drive to do better in life gave me the extra push that I needed. I would communicate to my dad what my passions were, what I like to do, and he would give me ideas about how to take those passions and turn them into a dream come true. For example, I really enjoy studying controversial topics, doing research and writing about them. His interpretation of that was, you should write books. My mother has told me many times that I was a good writer and one day I will write books, but it wasn't until my Daddy suggested it and open the door that I actually went for it. Without any doubt, my dad is one of the main reasons that you read the words in this book, the reason I finished my first degree and the reason I decided to go into a career in social work. He may not have been there to witness me walk the stage, but he has certainly become my coach in the corner.

Daddiless daughters, you may feel that no one is there to be your coach or affirm you, but I would like to encourage you! As discussed earlier God is your father and if you listen for him he will tell you exactly what he made you to be! You may not have a relationship with God, but those ideas, dreams and goals could very much be your daddy in heaven whispering messages to you about who he made you to be, what career you should take up and even what business to start. Just know that if you don't get that affirmation directly from your earthly father, your heavenly Father will send it directly to you from his very own mouth! Now that is a deal!

CHAPTER SIX

Adult Relationships

"My Intervener"

After I ended my very toxic relationship of 6 years, I had a very healthy conversation with myself. I really wanted to know why we hooked up? Why did it last so long? What was the take-away lesson? At this point I had gotten over the "hurt" and had already reconstructed my life without him. It is my belief and conviction that if you don't learn the lesson you were supposed to learn from a bad breakup it will happen again. So, I came to this conclusion. We got together to fill a void we were both missing, and we stayed together because we had become codependent on each other. He gave me the attention and affection that I didn't know I was missing from my dad and I gave him the love, care and nurturing that he didn't get from his mother. What a disaster! He had mother wounds and I had an absent father and together we made a dysfunctional mess. Our relationship in short was the equivalent of trying to mix oil and water, try as you may it WILL NOT come together. The most important lesson that I learned is that it takes two whole people, not two broken people to make for a healthy relationship. Relationships are about what you can contribute to the other person's life, but if you are not complete within yourself it becomes all about what you can get out of them.

A dating relationship is defined as an interpersonal relationship that involves physical and/or emotional intimacy such as romantic love or sexual activity. As mentioned earlier there is a chain reaction a woman goes through in a search for love.

First in the father and if he isn't present, then it trickles to the mother and if she can't give it then a woman will search for it in relationships. At this point a woman has moved out of her childhood and adolescent years and into adulthood all without a father. Somewhere in her subconscious are those deep standing father wounds. In a relationship, after the newness and excitement has worn off, Daddiless daughters may start placing high expectations on their lover to give them the love lost in childhood. "The fact is, these childhood/adolescent needs for love do not belong in her adult love relationships" (Thomas, 2014). On the contrary daughters who were well fathered are "more apt to have the kinds of skills and attitudes that lead to more fulfilling relationships with men" (Nelson 2014). One author suggests that a woman's early experiences with her father have a link to the experiences she will have in her relationships with men (Jackson, 2010). In essence there are two major concerns with relationships as it pertains to Daddiless daughters that we will discuss. First off, Daddiless daughters tend to have lower standards, which could lead them to being involved in toxic relationships. Secondly, on the other end of the spectrum there are those that date or become "unavailable loves".

Toxic Relationships

Low self-esteem and low standards almost undoubtedly go hand in hand! When a woman with low self-esteem enters a relationship, she is at a great risk for being subject to mistreatment and even abuse. This is mostly due to her compelling desire to have the love she is longing for causing her to settle for less than what she deserves. How many times do we see women who work hard, get her own house, her own car and her man on the other hand is depending on her resources. Truth is she deserves so much more, but no man was there to give a standard. You see, fathers teach their daughters what to expect from a man and set the standards for who they should date. "What's surprising is not that fathers have such an impact on their daughters' relationships with men, but that they generally have more impact than mothers do" (Nelson). That is not only a mouth full, but for Daddiless daughters that could be hard pill to swallow.

Low standards and bad decisions will land a woman right in the hands of a codependent lover and a toxic relationship. Among the different types of toxic relationships are verbal, physical, emotional, mental or financial abuse. We see women who want to "take care" of their lovers and then there are those who are being abused by them. "The semi-conscious hope is that she will take care of a lover well enough that he will be able to return the favor at some point later on"

(Thomas). This is really an effort to rehabilitate someone into being the man that will satisfy her childhood needs. Most domestic violence cases stem from relationships like this! Many people looked at a woman in an abusive relationship and wonder, why won't she just leave him! Here is my take, there is a fear of abandonment there, she is first off afraid that this man will leave her like her daddy did. This fear of abandonment leads to what's known as self-silencing which makes them less likely to leave the relationship. "Fatherless women tend to cling to their partners in a suffocating manner in fear these men will abandon them as their fathers once did" (Rowlette, 2013).

I can remember a time when I pleaded with my ex-boyfriend not to leave me. Where did all that come from? I mean I was doing well for myself, I was doing great in college, I had my own car, I had my own apartment, and great friends. I didn't need him for anything at all. We lived together as "roommates" and when we would get into a real heated argument, he would threaten to leave while I was at work or at school. Now, I know why it was such a painful thought! One day I went to elementary school and came home, and my daddy was GONE! I subconsciously was afraid to relive that moment again. Today I am proud to say that I found a man that says he will NEVER leave me or forsake me, he promised to be with me even unto the end of the earth. He not only shows me love, but he is love! Yes, here I go again talking about my Man upstairs!

UNAVAILABLE LOVERS

Yet another form of a toxic relationship is what's known as an unavailable lover. That is to say that a woman has identified with the unavailability of their father and thus pick up men who are also unavailable (Thomas, 2012). This is seen a lot in women whose fathers were present physically in the household but not emotionally. In other words, they pretty much go to work, come home sit in front of a television eating dinner and never once acknowledge their child. Fathers like this are detached from their children and families, they don't communicate much, and they don't show any emotions towards their daughters. The conversations between them and their daughters are very few and far in between and awkward to say the least. Fathers who are deceased, unknown or uninvolved and not present can also be considered unavailable. It may seem masculine to be emotionally detached but your silence as a father is also a teacher. Daughters who experienced fathers like this may find themselves in a relationship with an unavailable lover. He may not return phone calls, text or even interact with your family and friends, he may not even spend quality time with you as his significant other. Of course, for a Daddiless daughter who had an unavailable father that is all too normal. In the same way that a woman can date an unavailable lover, she herself can become one. She may be the one who is distant and detached, just like her daddy!

No matter what the terms of the relationships are, unhealthy relationships are closely related to the absences of a daddy. An interesting study test and compared the cortisol levels of fatherless daughters with girls who had fathers. People with low cortisol tend to be more sensitive and overactive to stress. Coincidentally the low cortisol group was found the be the Daddiless daughters. These daughters with low cortisol also described their relationships with men as stressful in terms of rejection, unpredictability or coercion (Nelson, 2014).

I would like to encourage you! Your real Father is not the author of confusion and he is a very present help in a time of need. He actually insists that you communicate with him, so much so that he tells you to cast ALL your cares on Him because he cares for you!

CHAPTER SEVEN

Marriage

"My Exchanger"

In a tradition wedding ceremony, the bride groom and wedding party stand in expectation waiting for the entrance of the bride. The bride appears beautiful and radiant on the arms of her very first love, her daddy. Once the bride and her father have walked the isle, her daddy gently hands her off to the bride groom with a little hesitation and a whole lot of confidence at the *altar.* Have you ever considered why it is the father, and not the mother that gives a daughter's hand in marriage? I believe that it is God's design that a woman in all her femininity goes from one "covering" of protection and provision to another, never being left without covering. A wedding is really, symbolic of the great exchange happening! In ancient middle eastern culture and religion, it was a custom for the fathers to arrange marriages for their children. The father of the groom would pay a price for his son to marry and the father of the bride would receive that payment. Often, the bride's father would give her a portion of the what he receives and if he was rich he would also give her property and maidservants. Essentially the bride's former estate is losing a household member and the family of the groom is gaining one. When considering a possible mate for his daughter, a father would take into account several factors. Those are: the reputation of the family, the family vocation (the more prestigious the better), wealth, appearance, values, religion and medical history (Zuffoletti, 2007). It is apparent that in those days, the father played a major role in who their daughter should marry. Today, it is said that a father plays just as much of a role now, if not more than in the old days, which may be hard to believe. In our modern western culture, it is not arranged marriage that gives our fathers the ability to choose who we marry; but it's the impact they have or don't have on our lives that influences the decisions of the bride. That may sound a little bit depressing, but there is good news!

    While there is sufficient evidence to prove that dating and relationships are affected by not having a father, there is a lot less evidence that suggest that marriages are also affected. In fact, one study concluded that "there was very little consistent evidence of negative effects on marriages or divorce..." (Mclanahan, 2013). Here the author explains how there has been no real statistics that show any correlation between absent fathers and marriage. On another note "girls who had fathers are less likely to become sexually active early which leads to waiting to get married and have children (Nelson, 2014). Girls who had fathers are also said to have better relationships with men in general. This is to say that girls who didn't have fathers may have suffered some loss in the area of marriage. How are these concepts consistent from childhood all the way through the relationship period but not marriage? Well there are a few possible reasons why... Perhaps at this stage of a woman's life she has learned to accept the absence of her father and live with the man that she has. Maybe it is because less emphasis is being placed on marriage as compared to previous generations; therefore, statistics reflect a smaller demographic of people. It could be possible that specifically Daddiless daughters are not marrying, for obvious reasons.

    As mentioned earlier, marriage is about an exchange taking place. Many women around the world are faced with the challenge of not having anyone to hand them off in marriage. It's more than just having a daddy walk you down the aisle at a wedding. It's about having the years of experience being nurtured, loved, protected and provided for by the head of her household. In a perfect situation, a woman picks a man that is actually worth marrying and learns how to be loved by a man the right way. It doesn't take science to tell us that, this scenario could turn out more ways than one. We could point out all the possibilities of what a marriage would look like for Daddiless daughters or rule out their ability to maintain a healthy marriage or determine whether their marriage will or will not end in divorce. However, I don't think that would makes a real difference either way. I choose to remain optimistic and believe that informed women can make informed decisions in a marriage. It is my hope that women, after reading this book would evaluate whether or not they have truly dealt with the impact of not having a father. A wound properly diagnosed and treated will heal. With healing comes the ability to love and be loved the right way.

I'll close with this:

Earlier in this chapter I mention how the exchange that happens between the father and bride groom takes place at the altar. I would like to encourage you that the natural father wasn't the only father present in the wedding. The altar is symbolic of the place where God Himself receives a sacrifice. That means that God is present at the altar, alongside the groom receiving the commitment and sacrifice of marriage. I'm saying all that to say, if you don't or didn't have a natural father that can give you away at the wedding, God is there. Relying on God your father to exchange you is a good place to be. The natural father who arranges a marriage for his daughter would make sure that the potential spouse meets his qualifications. He would also, if he were rich provide the daughter with estates and inheritances when she leaves his house. How much more would your Father in Heaven who wants the absolute best for you not do the same and more. Maybe that's why the bible states "A man that finds a wife finds a good thing and obtains favor from the Lord". So, that means that when a man finds a wife he doesn't just get a good thing, but he gets favor from the Lord. You see as the bride's Father, God sends her off with favor and blessings and also being the grooms Father, God pays for the price of the bride for his son. Since there is no price for the daughters of God, he gives endless blessings and favor. The husband of a Daddiless daughter has got some big shoes to fill, not because she is so broken but because her Father is so GOOD! Fathers can give their sons an inheritance of houses and wealth, but only the Lord can give an understanding wife" Proverbs 19:14 (NLT).

Epilogue

In my first semester at Florida Atlantic University school of social work, I took a class called Issues in Counseling Women. One of the main assignments was to pick a topic of interest, write a ten-page paper on it and do a fifteen-minute presentation at the close of the semester. My first thought was, what in the world am I going to talk about. About half way through the semester, as the deadline was approaching, I had a conversation with a friend of mine that really opened my mind to a topic I really had never considered before. We were talking about dating and relationships, and I noticed that she had dated a lot of guys but had NO emotional attachment to them and had no problem dismissing them just as fast as they came. I asked her a question that would be the start of a new train of thought for me. The question I asked her was, what is your relationship like with your father? Her answer was astounding to me, and I thought, well I just made a new personal discovery! She said to me "me and my dad ain't close like that, I talk to him when I feel like it". Then I began to think about my own dating experiences and how they were affected by my dad's absence. I noticed that there was a correlation between how my friend viewed her dad and how she related to men she dated and even friends she had.

From there I began to do research on absent fathers, and I wrote the whole ten-page paper in just a few hours. At the close of the semester I turned my paper in and did my presentation and to my surprise I got a 100 percent on both the paper and the presentation! My teacher even decided to add this to her list of topics to discuss for the next semester. I was so thrilled I had to send a copy of the paper to my father in prison. He read the paper and began showing it to his fellow inmates and got some really great reviews about its content. My father suggested I write a book about it and even got me connected with a publisher, so I took his advice. It is my hope to not necessarily present to you a bunch of information, but to give you real life application on how this topic could be relevant to you or someone you know. Maybe you are a father in prison with daughters, like my father. Perhaps you are a single mother raising daughters, or a daughter without a dad for whatever reason. Or maybe you haven't been in your daughter's life, but you would like to be. You may even be married to a Daddiless daughter. Whatever the case is, I hope that you would find some insight and begin your own conversation that would lead to a deeper understanding and ultimately inner healing.

We have come to the end of our journey at exploring the lives of Daddiless Daughters. Overall, we see that fathers have a very dramatic effect on any girls' life. In many instances his absence could determine the course of her life. From the time a girl is an infant she is learning to connect with men through her connection with her father. At school aged dads encourage daughters to compete with "the big boys", in adolescent years a father teaches his daughter that she is "the most beautiful girl in the world" and in her relationships, dad is there to say, "don't take no junk off of him". But what happens to the girls that miss out on these opportunities? Many of them have a mother there to compensate for the loss, and those that don't might have some unfortunate outcomes. These outcomes vary from person to person and some women might not be affected at all. In any case, there is hope for every Daddiless daughter; by acknowledging the pain of not having a father, grieving over it if need be and finally letting it go! I love the way Dr. Cindy Trimm put it…she said "Everything your father needed to give you, you already have. Thank God for the 23 chromosomes that he contributed to you becoming the beautiful, amazing person you are!

    I've shared with you my person experience of being a Daddiless daughter. My father has been incarcerated for 16 years, a very large part of my childhood. The results for me effected many areas of my life like self-esteem, dating, career, and relationships. Since developing a richer relationship with my daddy I realized what a real man is supposed to be, do and say. I suppose that with my own personal experience it further validates the research I have done. My daddy always told me "Help someone however you can, whenever you can and where ever you can, and you will always be blessed". I hope something I have said in this book has helped you to either help yourself or help someone else.

Be Blessed!

References

Jackson, L. (2010). *Where's My Daddy? Effects of Fatherlessness on Women's Relational Communication.* Retrieved from http://scholarworks.sjsu.edu/cgi/viewcontent.cgi?article=4763&context=etd_theses

Nelson, L. (2014, June 3). *How Dads Affect their Daughters into Adulthood.* Retrieved from http://family-studies.org/how-dads-affect-their-daughters-into-adulthood/

Mancini, L. (2010, May 10). *Father Absence and its Effect on Daughters.* Retrieved from http://library.wcsu.edu/dspace/bitstream/0/527/1/Final+Thesis.pdf

McLanahan, S., Tach, L., & Schneider, D. (2013). The Causal Effects of Father Absence. Annual Review of Sociology, 399, 399–427. http://www.ncbi.nlm.nih.gov/pmc/articles/PMC3904543/

Rowlette, N. L. (2013 May 1). *A study of the relationship between adolescent female interpersonal development in a relationship and the influence of the absence of a father in the home.* Retrieved from http://digitalcommons.auctr.edu/cgi/viewcontent.cgi?article=1968&context=dissertations

The Huffington Post. *'Daddyless Daughters': How Growing up Without a Father Affects a Woman's Standard's and Choices.* Retrieved from http://www.huffingtonpost.com/2013/07/13/daddyless-daughters-standards-mistake-define_n_3587142.html

Thomas, J. (2012). *Absent Father and His Daughter's Love-Life.* Retrieved from http://lovelifelearningcenter.com/absent-father-his-daughters-love-life/

If you would like to have your book Published with **SOLMON & MAKEDA PUBLISHING,** contact us Today at
www.sm4publishing.com